Real Bosses Don't Say "Thank You"

A Guide To Being The Perfect Boss

Thanks are due to the following: my parents, Tom and Gert Nevins, and Rosalie La Grutta and Ed Winters, for endlessly proofreading and providing moral support; my co-workers, especially Sue Poremba and Steve Holt, for all of their suggestions and encouragement; Jim Harrison for his editing assistance and expertise; Jim Silady for his faith and financial support; Ellen Bordner for her patience and guidance; the staff of the Hillsborough Public Library for their help with the research; Tom Lenahan, Bob Shepherd, and Dick Woodbridge for their invaluable advice and assistance; and Mischa Richter for his delightful cartoons.

An original publication of *Pollyanna Press*

Pollyanna Press, a division of
Nevins Publishing Company
Suite 177
422 Route 206
Somerville, NJ 08876

ISBN: 0-914359-00-2

First Printing September 1983

Printed in the U.S.A.

Cover design by Ellen Nevins and Ellen Bordner

Contents

Contents

Contents

Contents

Author's Note

Throughout this book, I have referred to the Real Boss as a "he." This is because most of the Real Bosses of the world are, in fact, males: few females have held positions of real responsibility long enough to qualify. In time, however, it is expected that more and more women will graduate to the ranks of the Real Bosses—assuming, that is, that they *want* to.

Introduction

First came all the flap over the culinary preferences of what Bruce Feirstein alleges to be "Real Men." To hear Mr. Feirstein tell it, today's male has nothing more important to worry about than what he should have for lunch. Yet in view of today's unsettled interest rates and uncertain profits, this is just not true! As any successful businessman can tell you, the only men who have time to worry about such trivial matters as whether to eat quiche are those men who are so low on the corporate totem pole that their most important decision of the week concerns which team to bet on in the office football pool.

Those men who have any *real* responsibilities—those men who have the *real* decisions to make—just can't afford to spend their time worrying about what to eat for lunch. These men are far too busy channeling their energies into making decisions that will determine the well-being not only of themselves and their corporations but, ultimately, their country and the world. Surely no one believes that John DeLorean took the time to worry about whether he dare eat quiche as he watched his automobile company sink into receivership. And can anyone really imagine George Steinbrenner worrying about what to have for lunch when he's got to decide whether to hire—or fire—Billy Martin again?

But Mr. Feirstein is not the only one laboring under a gross misconception regarding a busy person's real concerns. For shortly after he misled us about "Real Men," Joyce Jillson got into the act with her assertion that "Real Women" don't pump gasoline—or otherwise attend to the maintenance of their own cars.

Unfortunately, Ms. Jillson, too, is living in the past. Gone are the days of *Pillow Talk* and *Gidget Goes Hawaiian:* now is the era of *Kramer vs. Kramer* and *An Unmarried Woman*. In view of today's high divorce rate and the ever-increasing number of single-parent families, women can no longer afford the luxury of being unable to fend for themselves. As a result, women have been flocking to the workplace in record numbers: today many women are just as much a part of the corporate rat race—and subject to the same strenuous demands— as are millions of men. These women don't have time to stand around haggling over who is going to fill the damned gas tank! What matters to today's woman is that the tank get filled in order that she can get to her next business meeting on time. Surely Sandra Day O'Connor would fill her own gas tank if she would otherwise miss hearing an important case. Why, in order to be present at Bill Agee's next takeover meeting, even Mary Cunningham would pump her own gas.

The time has come to set the record straight. Busy, responsible men and women in today's world really don't care who eats what for lunch, as long as these people take no longer than their allotted lunch period to do so. Nor do these men and women care who pumps the gasoline that powers their automobiles, as long as the price per gallon is the lowest one in town. These people aren't the least bit concerned with what it takes to be a "Real Man" or a "Real Woman." Instead, they want to know how best to meet the many and diverse demands of the corporate environment: how to discharge their corporate responsibilities, how to deal with their subordinates, how to survive in the hectic corporate world. In short, these people want to know what it takes to be a "Real Boss." It is for these concerned, conscientious, dedicated souls that this book has been written.

"Well, we <u>are</u> an equal opportunity employer."

Today's Real Boss

Until the end of the last century, it was relatively easy to be a "Real Boss." For one thing, there were few restrictions to contend with: you hired whomever you chose, you told these people what they were to do, you paid them a nominal wage to do it, and you fired them if they didn't do it correctly. Besides that, most workers were so grateful to be employed that they really didn't look to get anything out of their work other than a regular paycheck.

But times have changed drastically, and the corporate environment has mellowed considerably. Today's boss faces many demands on his time and decision-making prowess that were not there before. No longer is any boss free to hire whomever he chooses: today's boss must be mindful at all times of meeting his EEO quotas. Nor can today's boss fire anyone at will, lest he incur the wrath of a labor union or the ACLU. In addition, so secure is the modern employee that a weekly paycheck is no longer adequate compensation: today's employee wants "meaningful feedback" regarding his accomplishments, as well as plenty of opportunity for personal and professional "development"—not to mention a host of costly fringe benefits. On top of all this, the modern boss is still expected to maintain a high level of productivity and to make sure that everything continues to run in the black.

So what does it take to be a Real Boss today? How is it that the Real Boss responds to the numerous challenges facing him in the modern workplace? What qualities does the Real Boss possess that set him apart from ordinary bosses who attempt with so much less success to overcome today's endless obstacles to productivity? And how does the Real Boss prove himself when he's up against such constraints as OSHA regulations, the thirty-five hour work week, and the minimum wage? Actually, the answers to these questions are easy for anyone who's ever worked for a Real Boss.

The Real Boss is one who is in fact a *real boss*. The Real Boss does not for one minute allow his subordinates to rule the office. The Real Boss never forgets for a minute that *he* is in charge and that, ultimately, the responsibility for his entire organization rests solely upon *his* shoulders. And large though this responsibility may be, the Real Boss never takes it lightly, nor does he ever try to shirk it. Real Bosses do not hide behind such phrases as "participative management."

The Real Boss understands the value of tradition. He isn't tempted to try out each new management fad that comes along, nor does he read each new book about management theory. The Real Boss is secure in the knowledge that he's done fine for years just by doing things exactly the way he's still doing them. (Otherwise, he asserts, he would never have gotten to be a Real Boss in the first place.) The Real Boss knows he doesn't need a Ph.D. in Labor Relations to manage his people, just because it's suddenly fashionable to have one. Nor does he need an M.B.A. from Stanford to turn a profit.

The Real Boss believes in getting the job done. He also believes that this end justifies any means necessary to achieve it. The Real Boss does not lose sight of goals once they are set. The Real Boss is a man of actions rather than words. The Real Boss does not spend a lot of time talking about what must be done. He much prefers that this time be used to *do* it.

The Real Boss has no time for frivolity. The Real Boss takes the privilege of being a Real Boss very seriously. He expects his charges to take the privilege of working for a Real Boss equally seriously.

The Real Boss recognizes the importance of maintaining an appropriate image. Toward this end, the Real Boss knows how to be tough—on all matters and at all times. The Real Boss has no use for sentiment or sensitivity. He is not one to coddle his subordinates, or to provide these underlings with other "positive strokes." The Real Boss realizes that such actions would only encourage his charges to be soft. These actions also take up time and energy that can more profitably be channelled elsewhere.

In fact, those qualities which serve to make a Real Boss so distinctive can best be summed up in one short sentence: Real Bosses don't say "Thank you." The Real Boss knows that, even in today's world, having a steady job and getting paid on a regular basis should be thanks enough for his minions. The Real Boss also asserts that saying "Thank you" is a colossal waste of time! And while this may make him sound like something of an ingrate, in many ways he has a valid point. After all, the Great Pyramids still would not be complete if Ramses II had stopped to thank each of his slaves every time one of them moved a stone into place. And how far would Henry Ford have gotten if he had taken the time to thank each of his assemblers whenever one of them managed to slip a bolt into the proper slot?

Real Boss Review

Q: How many Real Bosses does it take to change a light bulb?

A: None. Real Bosses don't change light bulbs. Real Bosses know that's what underlings are for.

Debunking Some
Real Boss Myths

Now that you have some idea how a Real Boss differs from the plain vanilla variety, you are probably starting to wonder who some of the Real Bosses are. But before we actually identify those rare individuals who have qualified for Real Boss status, there are a few things you should know.

Contrary to what most people assume, Real Boss status is not a function of level, or rank. Real Boss status is mainly a function of attitude, or behavior. It's not how far you've gone that counts—it's how you've gotten wherever you are. Nor is it a question of how much power you hold; the key is how you wield whatever power you've got. It doesn't even matter how many underlings you claim. The crucial factor is how you treat the people you do control.

Another popular notion holds that Real Bosses are found only in the corporate world—and only in big companies at that. But this is just not true! The corporate community has certainly spawned more than its share of Real Bosses—most likely it is this type of Real Boss that *you* want to be. But not all of the Real Bosses of the world run around five days a week in gray flannel or navy pinstripes. Many Real Bosses are found in olive drab or khaki, with all sorts of stripes and stars and badges on their chests. And Real Bosses are often found in other kinds of uniforms as well. For Real Bosses can be found in the military, the sports world, the entertainment industry, and even in politics: wherever one person can be put in charge of another, a Real Boss can emerge.

In fact, there is probably not a single field of human endeavor that cannot claim at least one Real Boss to its credit. The mere fact that someone is not a part of the business world in no way prevents him from becoming a Real Boss. The size of his organization really doesn't matter, either. The only things that are absolutely essential to becoming a Real Boss are determination and the proper attitude: the willingness to learn—and to play by—all the Real Boss guidelines in this book.

"That will do, Miss Briggs. Now, make me a cup of coffee and take a letter."

Who's Who Among Real Bosses

I t takes a special kind of person to be today's Real Boss. You need the strategic ability of Knute Rockne, the iron fist of Margaret Thatcher, and the determination of Genghis Khan. Ideally, you will also have the stoicism of Marcus Aurelius, the drive of a turbo-charged Porsche 928, and the perseverance of The Little Engine That Could. *

So who are the ones who have made it? Who are the taskmasters, past and present, who have displayed the appropriate skills? Surely you've guessed the identities of some of these people by now. But if you're still looking for a few good role models, the following list should help.

---

* Actually, another highly desirable quality—at least from a subordinate's point of view—is the patience of Job. But, alas! Even a Real Boss can't have everything, and it is this quality Real Bosses usually elect to do without. Besides, in the immortal words of Osgood Fielding III, "Nobody's perfect."

Real Bosses

Lucretia Borgia
Oliver Cromwell
Jimmy Hoffa
Juan Peron
King Henry VIII
Ayatollah Khomeini
Attila the Hun
Eva Peron
Idi Amin
"Boss" Tweed
John D. Rockefeller
J. Edgar Hoover
King John
Ivan the Terrible
George Patton
Helena Rubinstein
Margaret Thatcher
Harold Geneen
J. Paul Getty
Yuri Andropov

Hernando Cortez
Cornelius Vanderbilt
Mao Tse Tung
Herod
Richard Daley
King George III
Henry Ford
Charles Revson
Lyndon Johnson
Caligula
Czar Nicholas II
"Papa Doc" Duvalier
Al Capone
George Steinbrenner
Armand Hammer
Richard Nixon
Leo Durocher
Nero
Henry Kissinger
Huey Long

The Real Boss's Creed

Ask not what you can do for your underlings.

Ask only what your underlings can do for you.

Bosses Who Will Never Be Real Bosses

Of course, not all of the well-known taskmasters of the world possess those very special qualities that are necessary to qualify for Real Boss status. By some strange quirk of fate, some people have managed to attain positions that give them considerable authority over others despite the fact that they are not suitably iron-fisted or aloof. These are the "bosses" who just don't seem to understand what human nature is and how it must be handled. These are the "softies," those misguided souls who allow compassion and concern to interfere with reason and resolve. In short, these are the bosses who say not only "Thank you," but also "Please" and "Hello."

The classic example of this kind of boss is Ed Koch, the mayor of New York City. It isn't bad enough that he greets his minions by name. This man goes so far as to ask his underlings what they think of his performance as mayor! You can be quite sure no Real Boss would ever do that. No Real Boss *cares* what his underlings think.

Mayor Koch also has the poor sense to engage in humor — on the job! He often makes wise cracks and witty remarks for others to hear. He's even been known to smile while performing his bossly duties—and in full view of his charges at that. There is virtually no hope of Ed Koch ever becoming a Real Boss. This man has never displayed even a minimal command of suitable Real Boss behavior.

Another good example is Leo Buscaglia, the "Love Doctor." His nickname alone tells you all you need to know about *this* man. No self-respecting Real Boss would ever allow a word like "love" to be used with *his* name. And this man's behavior violates every Real Boss rule in the book! He goes around hugging people, kissing them, patting them on the back—he does everything possible to encourage people to be *soft*. What kind of Real Boss would ever encourage that kind of behavior? Did Vince Lombardi go around kissing all of the Green Bay Packers whenever they lined up for a kickoff? Did George Patton hug each of his troops whenever they destroyed an enemy tank? Of course not! Yet these men got results! What kind of results has the "Love Doctor" ever gotten? And how can this man even *hope* to get any respect?

A third example is John Opel, Chairman of the Board of IBM. Granted, Mr. Opel *dresses* like a Real Boss—what IBMer doesn't? But he certainly doesn't *talk* like a Real Boss. No Real Boss would ever assert that, "You have to have people free to act, or they become dependent."* The Real Boss wants his subordinates to be dependent; how else will he ever control them? Nor would any Real Boss ever suggest of his charges, "They don't need to be told; they have to be allowed."* Among Real Bosses, this kind of talk is heresy! No Real Boss is going to "allow" anything if he can help it! What is the Real Boss for if not to *tell?* Besides, the Real Boss knows darned well that most of his subordinates wouldn't know what to do without being told.

*As quoted by John Flack in *Time*, July 11, 1983.

Surprisingly, there have been numerous other "bosses" over the years who have demonstrated equally unsuitable behavior — notables who, while they must be considered "bosses" by virtue of their authority over others, will never be included among the ranks of the Real Bosses. (Needless to say, these are also the people whose examples you want to avoid.)

The "Softies"

Adlai Stevenson
Pope John Paul II
Queen Elizabeth II
Casey Stengel
Theodore Hesburgh
Queen Juliana
Dwight Eisenhower
Millicent Fenwick
Ivan the Great
Don Shula
Yogi Berra
Dag Hammarskjold
Grant Tinker
Gene Autry
Sherry Lansing
Bob Hope
Dianne Feinstein
Catherine the Great

Constantine the Great
Tom Landry
Hubert Humphrey
Frank Borman
Mohandas Gandhi
Harry Truman
William Westmoreland
Sir Thomas More
Robert E. Lee
Queen Victoria
Fiorello LaGuardia
Charles L. Brown
Omar Bradley
Frank Reynolds
George C. Marshall
John R. Bennett
Beverly Sills
Joe Paterno

Real Boss
Words of Wisdom #1

"Nice guys finish last."

—Leo Durocher

Bosses Who Think They're Real Bosses When They're Not

Unfortunately, there are also those bosses who think they're Real Bosses when, in fact, they are not. These are the people who exhibit some of the appropriate behavior all of the time—or all of the appropriate behavior some of the time—yet continually fall short of the mark.

For example, despite his fervent assurances that he was "in control," Alexander Haig has never qualified —and he probably never will. Real Bosses do not surrender their power without a fight! (Although it must be conceded that anyone who can command $25,000 for a single speaking engagement is definitely doing *something* right.)

Mary Cunningham hasn't made it, either—although she may well make it yet. For she is not likely to stop until she gets what she wants. Besides, if all else fails, she can always cozy up to the right person.

And these two are not alone in their lack of success. Other notables who think they're Real Bosses when they're not include:

Teri Shields
Joan Rivers
John Dean III
Jane Fonda
Helen Gurley Brown

Phyllis Schlafly
Howard Cosell
Pete Rose
Dr. Joyce Brothers
Jane Byrne

"Grandfather, Dad, Members of the Board."

Real Boss Demeanor

The Real Boss recognizes the importance of maintaining the proper distance between himself and his subordinates at all times. This is essential if he is to preserve an atmosphere of suitable objectivity. If he allows familiarity of any kind to develop, the Real Boss knows that his charges will think he is weak. In turn, they will inevitably try to take advantage of this weakness and use it to further their own ends.

In order to maintain an appropriate distance, the Real Boss always displays a suitable demeanor. This means that he acts as follows:

1. The Real Boss never displays any friendliness toward his charges. Not only does he shun all social interactions with these people but, most of the time, he doesn't even address them by name. (In fact, half the time, he can't remember their names.) Nor does he bother to acknowledge their presence when he comes upon them in the hall. (Besides, the Real Boss wonders, what are they doing in the hall? Why aren't they at their desks doing their work?)

2. A Real Boss is equally unfriendly to all his subordinates. The Real Boss foresees the consequences of

inconsistency on this matter. If he is even slightly more pleasant or agreeable toward one underling than toward another, he is likely to be accused of favoritism—and that can lead to bad morale. The Real Boss certainly doesn't want any morale problems among his people. That could lessen their productivity.

3. Real Bosses never admit there is anything they do not know. The Real Boss acts as though he knows all things about all subjects at all times. If he does not have all the facts or is not entirely sure of an answer, the Real Boss knows to bluff. (All Real Bosses can do this well. In fact, that's how most of them got to be Real Bosses in the first place.) And the Real Boss doesn't worry about anyone detecting this bluff. For one thing, he doubts that any of his charges are quite that smart. But even if he does get caught, the Real Boss can cover himself: he can bluff again—more convincingly this time.

4. Real Bosses never apologize for anything. After all, being a Real Boss means never having to say you're sorry. The Real Boss is exempt from the need to express any regret by virtue of the fact that he *is* a Real Boss: as such, he is entitled to say and do things for which lesser mortals—such as his underlings—would need to apologize.

5. Real Bosses never express gratitude in any form. The Real Boss knows that his underlings are paid— and paid well by his reckoning—to do whatever they do. No further expression of gratitude is ever necessary. Besides, if he expresses his gratitude verbally, the Real Boss knows that his charges

will only come to expect some more tangible form of thanks. No Real Boss encourages expectations of this sort. Underlings are not supposed to have expectations. Only Real Bosses are allowed to have expectations of any kind.

6. Real Bosses never tolerate humor on the job. The Real Boss has too much work to do—and takes this work too seriously— to have any time for frivolity. Being a Real Boss is no laughing matter! The Real Boss never even smiles on company time, nor does he encourage his charges to do so. (In fact, he is immediately suspicious of any person who *does* smile. Doesn't this person have enough work to do? Doesn't he take his work seriously?) Besides, the Real Boss knows that laughing and smiling require expenditures of energy that could better be used for other things.

7. The Real Boss never expresses any compassion or concern. He never takes any interest in an underling as a person, a unique human being. The Real Boss knows that these sentiments are completely out of place within any kind of business environment. He pays his people to do a job, not to bring their problems into the office. The only concern any Real Boss expresses regarding his charges is whether they have done their work—and if not, why not?

8. The Real Boss never admits that he is wrong. Fortunately, he never *is* wrong.

"Frown."

Expressions the Real Boss Loves to Use

"You're late."

"You're wrong."

"You're fired."

"That's not what I wanted."

"That's not how I wanted it."

"Do it over."

"I need it by 5:00."

"You'll have to cancel your dinner plans for this evening."

"You'll have to cancel your vacation plans for next week."

Expressions the Real Boss Hates to Use

"Good morning."

"Good night."

"You're early."

"You're right."

"You did a good job."

"That's a good idea."

Expressions
the Real Boss
Refuses to Use

"I was wrong."
"I'm sorry."
"How'm I doing?"
"Please."
"Thank you."

How the Real Boss Makes Decisions

How a boss handles the decision-making process is a vital clue to whether he is in fact a Real Boss. All Real Bosses always stick to certain clearly defined procedures whenever they have to make a decision of any kind.

For example, the Real Boss always puts off making any decision for as long as possible. He justifies this behavior on the grounds that it gives him time to acquire and digest all the information he needs to make the decision intelligently. This strategy also increases the likelihood that something will happen to render the decision unnecessary. If something like that *does* happen, the Real Boss is then free to concentrate his efforts on getting his job done. He also runs less risk of making a wrong decision.

When the Real Boss has reached the point of no possible further procrastination, he always makes the decision totally, entirely, and completely by himself. The Real Boss knows better than to allow any subordinate to participate in this decision in any way, regardless of the nature of the decision. After all, the Real Boss is the only person with enough perspective to make the *right* decision. No underling can possibly be objective enough to help make decisions that might in some way affect his career — or any other major aspect of

his life. If an underling were qualified to make these decisions, he wouldn't be an underling—he'd be a Real Boss.

Once the Real Boss has made a decision, he knows
better than to give his subordinates any reasons for this
decision. The Real Boss realizes that it is his prerogative
to make any decision he chooses without having to answer to his underlings. Besides, if he gives his employees
a reason for one decision, they're likely to expect to be
given reasons for other decisions as well. And that could
cause some big problems for the Real Boss: if he gets
into the habit of giving reasons, whatever will he do
when he has no reasons?

Most importantly, once he has made a decision,
the Real Boss knows to stick to this decision at all costs.
The decision must be upheld even in the very unlikely
event that it turns out to be completely wrong. After
all, sticking with a decision even when it's dead wrong
shows great consistency and determination. And, an
admission of error is likely to cost the Real Boss the respect of his underlings. He knows how important it is
to these people to be able to see him as perfect.

"I'll get back to you on that."

Rules and Company Policy

Every Real Boss understands the importance of observing company policy to the letter at all times. It may be true that rules were made to be broken, but the Real Boss will be damned if they're going to be broken by any of *his* charges.

This is largely because the Real Boss has no use for "flexibility." All Real Bosses know that "flexibility" is just a fancy name for a lack of resolve. And every Real Boss realizes that this is a trait that just cannot be tolerated in a Real Boss—although it is certainly a desirable quality for one's subordinates to have.

In addition, the Real Boss knows that rules impose a sense of order and continuity, which are two things he wants his organization to have. The Real Boss also knows that if he makes an exception to one rule for one person, he will then be expected to make an exception to some other rule for somebody else. If he's only going to end up making all these exceptions, he might as well not even have his rules in the first place. Yet if he doesn't have these rules, the Real Boss will never know how he is supposed to handle things.

Accordingly, the Real Boss never breaks any rules for anybody under any circumstances—unless, of course, he chooses to break them for himself. *

---

* It should be noted, however, that among Real Bosses this practice is not considered "rule-breaking." Instead, it is called "invoking executive privilege."

The
Real Boss's
Motto

Bureaucracy is beautiful.

Committees and the Real Boss

Every Real Boss is fully aware of the many benefits to be gained through the proper use of committees, task forces, and other kinds of deliberative panels. And while he doesn't believe in allowing his charges to participate in the decision-making process, he has no qualms about allowing these people to serve on committees—even when these committees are expected to make decisions of some kind.

Granted, this may seem like something of a contradiction—but it really isn't.

For one thing, the Real Boss knows that serving on committees will provide his subordinates with an excellent opportunity to acquire patience and frustration tolerance. And these are qualities that far too few people in the business world possess—though this is certainly not to suggest that the Real Boss doesn't have them.

Secondly, the Real Boss has been around long enough to realize that the smallest problem will be turned into a major dilemma—one that completely defies resolution—if it is assigned to a large enough committee. Therefore, the Real Boss knows that there is little danger of his charges doing any real decision-making while serving on these panels—for rarely do these groups actually make any decisions.*

---

* The Real Boss supports this argument by pointing to the record of the U. S. Congress — and the U.N.

"The last time I heard from him, he had just been assigned to a committee."

The Real Boss
and the Delegation
of Authority

Rarely does the Real Boss delegate any *real* authority. In the first place, the Real Boss sees the delegation of authority as the moral equivalent of copping out. How else can you describe a situation in which the Real Boss palms off his responsibilities onto someone else? And copping out is something no Real Boss wants to be accused of doing.

Besides, the Real Boss asserts that no one else is as well qualified to exercise his authority as he is. Nor is anyone else capable of exercising it as well.

However, there are times when the Real Boss absolutely must delegate authority—such as when a really important deadline has to be met and he has a big golf game scheduled, or when the task in question involves doing something the Real Boss doesn't like to do. In these instances, the Real Boss always makes sure that he delegates this authority to the person who is least qualified to handle it.

The Real Boss tells himself that this will give that person a good opportunity to become a bit more qualified. The Real Boss also surmises that this person is the one who is least likely to do so good a job at whatever he has been authorized to do that he is viewed as a serious contender for the Real Boss's job.

Murphy's Advice to Real Bosses

When in doubt, mumble.
When in trouble, delegate.

Real Boss Communications Policies

The ability to communicate effectively with one's charges is essential to being a Real Boss. The Real Boss must know just *what* to communicate to his charges. He also must know *when* and *how*.

For instance, the Real Boss knows to share with an underling only that information which is related directly —and exclusively—to that person's job. The Real Boss realizes that his charges have no need to know anything about what is going on elsewhere within the corporation. They need to know only those things that will help them get their own jobs done. It's best not to tell them too much anyway, so they don't get confused—or worried.

The Real Boss knows that his underlings don't want to be bothered about all sorts of trivial matters. In fact, they appreciate being spared all of the nonessential details, since this leaves them free to concentrate their energies on their work.

Even the essential information is best kept from one's charges for as long as possible. This, too, leaves them free to concentrate on their work. For example, all Real Bosses know that, if they tell a subordinate he's about to be transferred to another city, his mind will become cluttered with all sorts of useless nonsense that has nothing to do with getting his job done. He'll be too busy worrying about all sorts of little personal things—where he'll live, what interest rate he'll have to pay on his new mortgage, where his kids will go to school—to really be able to do his job right.

As proof of this point, the Real Boss looks to Reggie Jackson. Could Reggie possibly have played so well in the '81 Series if he had known that George Steinbrenner wasn't going to sign him on again the following spring? Of course not! He would have been too busy worrying about how to transfer all his cars— and transistor radios, and candy bars, and sports goggles, and money—out to California.

So, the Real Boss keeps even things like this to himself for as long as possible—say, up until the day before the transfer is effective. This may inconvenience his underlings a bit, but the Real Boss isn't too concerned about that.

Besides, he insists, any of his charges who are really interested in what's going on can generally find things out through the grapevine. So why should he make a point of telling them? After all, he asserts, no one had to tell Richard Nixon about the Watergate break-in. And did anyone have to tell Spiro Agnew about corruption in Maryland? Does anyone have to tell Mary Cunningham what "power hungry" means?

"The only things you need to know are those things
that will help you get your own job done."

Real Boss Motivation Strategies

F our thousand years after the Pharaohs took to flogging their slaves, the Real Bosses of the world are still faced with the difficult task of finding effective ways to motivate their subordinates. Fortunately, the methods used by Real Bosses today are much more humane than the methods used in ancient Egypt — and far more subtle.

The Real Boss no longer relies on the threat of physical violence to motivate his people. Today's Real Boss understands the value of psychology.

The modern Real Boss knows that the best way to motivate his charges is to show them how they stand to benefit from getting the job done. Every Real Boss knows that little incentives—such as the prospect of keeping one's job—often work wonders.

Only if this strategy fails will the modern Real Boss resort to the use of brute force.

Real Boss
Words of Wisdom #2

"It is far safer to be feared than loved."

—Niccolo Machiavelli

How the Real Boss
Assigns Jobs

One of the most difficult tasks facing any boss is deciding which person should get what job. Fortunately, the Real Boss knows just how to determine which job should go to each of his charges.

First, the Real Boss decides which of his underlings is most qualified for a particular job. Once he has identified this person, the Real Boss excludes him or her from further deliberation and goes on to consider each of his other charges. All other factors being equal, the Real Boss generally assigns the job to one of those underlings who is least qualified for it.

The Real Boss follows this procedure for several reasons. For one thing, he wants to be fair: he wants each of his subordinates to have an equal shot at every job opening. He knows that the most qualified person already has a distinct advantage over his peers in terms of qualifications for the job. Giving the job to this person will only give him a greater advantage, for he will become even more qualified for the job by virtue of the experience gained by doing the job. So, the Real Boss gives the job to some other subordinate in order to allow this person to put himself at less of a disadvantage by becoming more qualified. Since the least qualified people are the ones who are at the biggest disadvantage, it's only logical that the Real Boss should give the job to one of them.

Besides, the Real Boss knows that any person who is highly qualified for one particular job must be completely lacking in the skills required for most other jobs. After all, only Real Bosses are good at all things. Therefore, the Real Boss asserts, this underling should be given a job requiring proficiency in some of *those* skills. This will give this person just the opportunity he needs to overcome *his* deficiency.

"From now on, Watkins, you're <u>our</u> designated hitter."

Real Boss
Evaluations

No boss is quicker than the Real Boss to acknowledge the need for periodic evaluations of each of his subordinates. As time-consuming as these evaluations are, the Real Boss knows that they are essential if he is to stay abreast of how—and what—each of his underlings is doing. The Real Boss also knows that there are several key factors which must be weighed carefully in making these evaluations.

The first of these factors is the employee's attitude toward his job. In considering this, the Real Boss pays close attention to several tell-tale clues. The most important clue is the degree to which the subordinate is in agreement with the Real Boss. After all, the frequency with which an underling agrees or disagrees with the Real Boss says a great deal about that person's judgment and discretion. Any underling who is so lacking in discretion as to continually disagree with the Real Boss certainly does not have good enough judgment to merit commendation of any sort.

The second thing the Real Boss considers in evaluating someone is how well-rounded that person is. The Real Boss knows that being well-rounded is crucial to getting ahead. He also knows that being well-liked is one important component of being well-rounded. So, in order to assess how well-rounded a person is, the Real

Boss considers how well-liked this person is—as indicated by how much the Real Boss himself likes him. (The Real Boss has no doubt that this is a valid indication of how likeable that person really is. Being a good judge of character is a prerequisite for being a Real Boss.)

The last thing the Real Boss considers is the employee's actual job performance—how well this person has discharged those duties and responsibilities that are assigned to him. In assessing this, the Real Boss pays close attention to the neatness of the underling's desk. If the desk is consistently neat, the Real Boss rests assured that this person is getting his work done in a timely fashion. In addition, the Real Boss knows that a neat and tidy desk is usually a sign of an orderly mind—something he is always glad to see. On the other hand, if an employee's desk is consistently cluttered, the Real Boss can only conclude that the underling is *not* getting his work done. And a cluttered desk is a sure sign of a disordered mind.

"Knock it off, Watkins! You know how I feel
about cluttered desks!"

Real Boss
Feedback

Every Real Boss knows that he must provide his subordinates with feedback regarding their performance on the job. However, he also knows better than to provide this feedback on an ongoing basis. The Real Boss prefers to give all feedback to an underling at once, when the underling receives the results of his annual appraisal.

It's not that the Real Boss is too lazy to give feedback more often. It's just that he thinks feedback has more impact if it's given all at once. When it comes as a total surprise, the underling is unlikely to forget it.

Besides, the Real Boss theorizes that anyone who is doing a good job is probably aware of that fact without having to be told. So why should the Real Boss waste the time needed to tell him? Anyone who is not doing a good job obviously doesn't really care about his performance anyway—otherwise, he would be doing better. So why give him suggestions for improvement, or the chance to improve?

When the Real Boss finally does give an underling some feedback, he is careful not to praise this underling too highly or to give him too much credit for anything. The Real Boss knows that giving a subordinate a lot of positive feedback might encourage him to expect some sort of compensation for whatever he has done well enough to merit these accolades. And this can create some real problems. For when this compensation is not forthcoming—and it won't be—the employee is likely to feel frustrated and disappointed. This, in turn, is likely to demotivate the employee, and discourage him from continuing to do so well whatever he had done so well in the first place.

On those rare occasions when he can't find some way to completely avoid praising an underling, the Real Boss does at least make sure that this commendation is not given in front of the underling's peers. The Real Boss knows that praising one subordinate in front of others will only serve to demoralize these other people. This, in turn, is likely to demotivate *them*. Rather than risk the decrease in productivity that would inevitably result from this chain of events, the Real Boss wisely refrains from praising anyone publicly.

However, the fact that the Real Boss knows not to be too lavish with credit and praise does not deter him from doling out criticism and blame in generous measure. The Real Boss knows that this will keep his subordinates on their toes: it will keep them from becoming so satisfied with their work that they risk sinking into complacency. Liberal doses of castigation will also motivate his employees to work that much harder in order to avoid any further censure.

And while he knows never to commend a subordinate in front of the underling's peers, the Real Boss is quick to see the value of chewing out this person in front of these same peers. The Real Boss knows that there are many benefits to be gained by embarrassing an employee at every possible opportunity. If an underling is sufficiently embarrassed, he will take every step necessary to avoid doing again whatever he did to bring about this humiliation. The Real Boss also knows that this kind of public criticism serves as a good example: it provides fair warning to his other subordinates that they should avoid making whatever mistake prompted this embarassment — unless they want to receive the same treatment.

Regardless of whether he criticizes an underling privately or in public, the Real Boss knows never to explain why something was wrong or to give any suggestions as to how it might have been done differently. The Real Boss prefers to let his charges figure out for themselves just why something was wrong and what would have been correct. If a person has to figure these things out for himself, the Real Boss theorizes, he'll be that much less likely to ever make the same mistake again.

Real Boss
Words of Wisdom #3

"Don't get mad, get even."

—Joseph Patrick Kennedy

The Real Boss
and Salaries

When it comes to the issue of salaries, all Real Bosses share the same opinion: modern society attaches far too much significance to how much money one makes. Every Real Boss knows that money per se just isn't all that important. No amount of money could possibly equate with the tremendous satisfaction to be gained from getting one's job done.

Therefore, when his charges get their jobs done, the Real Boss asserts that these people should be content. After all, if they are going to experience all this satisfaction, they certainly can't hope to receive a lot of money too. On the other hand, if these people don't get their jobs done, they probably won't experience much satisfaction at all. But, under these circumstances, the Real Boss alleges that they have no right to expect a great deal of money either. Accordingly, the Real Boss always pays his minions as little as the traffic will bear. (Besides, the Real Boss muses, at least these people have jobs. Just how fussy can they be about how much money they make?)

With regard to raises, the Real Boss avoids giving these whenever possible. Every Real Boss knows that giving raises only serves to reduce his profit margin. What's worse, giving raises also contributes to inflation, since raises give people that much more money to pump into the economy. And inflation increases operating costs for the Real Boss, which only reduces his profit margin that much further. This, in turn, increases the likelihood that the whole organization will end up going bankrupt. In the interests of his underlings' job security, the Real Boss conscientiously avoids giving raises to any of his charges.

In those instances where the Real Boss absolutely must give someone a raise, he always monitors the amount of this raise very carefully. The Real Boss goes to great lengths to ensure that none of his charges receives too large a raise. If these things come too easily, the Real Boss reasons, his people won't bother to work very hard.

The Real Boss is especially careful never to let any of his subordinates receive a larger raise than *he* receives. The Real Boss knows that the biggest raises should always go to the Real Bosses, since *they* are the ones with the biggest responsibilities.

Real Boss
Words of Wisdom #4

"Happiness is positive cash flow."

—Frederick Adler

Absence and Vacation Policies

Real Bosses do not believe in "sick time." The Real Boss knows that truly conscientious, responsible underlings do not get sick.

Even if by chance some of his charges do become ill, the Real Boss does not feel that this justifies their spending time away from their assigned tasks. After all, the Real Boss reports for duty even when he has a temperature of 102°. Why shouldn't his subordinates do likewise?

Real Bosses make it very clear that they will not tolerate an underling taking time off just because he or some member of his family has been careless enough to come down with something. Only if a subordinate has died will this person be excused from his or her duties for reasons of ill health.

The Real Boss is only slightly more tolerant of those underlings who insist upon taking time off for a vacation.

The Real Boss knows that no truly dedicated underling ever uses up all of his allotted vacation time. The really conscientious employee simply will not be able to tear himself away for two or more weeks each year, so eager will he be to stay on top of things at the office.

As to when his charges actually may take their vacations—assuming some of them insist upon doing so—the Real Boss knows that he alone is qualified to decide just when these people need to do so. Accordingly, he plays an active role in determining when his underlings may and may not take time off.

And once these dates have been established, the Real Boss makes sure that each of these scheduled vacations is postponed at least once—preferably at the very last minute. This will ensure that his underlings appreciate their vacations that much more when they finally do get to take them. It will also serve to remind these people as to just who is in charge.

"What do you mean you're 'calling in sick'? Let me see
your tongue."

Promotions and the Real Boss

Promotions are a real sore spot with the Real Boss. Getting ahead is a great privilege, a rare reward— something no Real Boss will allow anyone to take for granted. Yet the Real Boss knows that people who are allowed to move ahead too quickly are likely to consider this kind of advancement to be their due. So, the Real Boss keeps a watchful eye on the speed at which his subordinates advance through the corporate ranks. He always makes sure they progress at a suitable pace—which means no faster than *he* did.

The Real Boss knows that his underlings benefit from this policy, for it keeps them humble. If they aren't allowed to advance too quickly, these people aren't likely to acquire an inflated sense of self-worth. While there's certainly no place for anything like humility in a Real Boss, this is definitely a virtue all underlings should possess.

Deep down inside, the Real Boss realizes that he, too, benefits from this policy. In the short run, he saves money by not having to fork out higher salaries. In the long run, the benefits are even greater: this policy ensures that it will be that much longer before any of his charges are in a position to challenge him for the job of Real Boss. *

* He realizes that none of them could really be worthy of the position— but the Real Boss is not one to take unnecessary risks.

Real Boss
Words of Wisdom #5

"Power is the great aphrodisiac."

—Henry Kissinger

Real Boss Grievance Procedures

Grievances rarely arise among those people who work for Real Bosses. How could anyone who is lucky enough to serve under a Real Boss possibly have any complaints? Besides, the Real Boss goes to great lengths to prevent grievances. But even if a grievance does come up, the Real Boss knows precisely how to handle it.

For starters, the Real Boss knows better than to encourage his charges to express any views contrary to his own, or to otherwise assert themselves in any manner. These people aren't being paid to express their views, the Real Boss reasons; they're being paid to do a job. Only an insubordinate subordinate would dare to challenge a Real Boss anyway—and no Real Boss has time to concern himself with people like this.

After all, the Real Boss knows all about "attitude problems"—he is quick to recognize one of these the minute it rears its ugly head. And any subordinate who expresses a gripe of any kind must in fact have an "attitude problem." What else could possibly be wrong? Surely his dissatisfaction can have nothing to do with the way the Real Boss runs the organization. The Real Boss knows he is a fair boss: how else could he ever have gotten to be a Real Boss? The Real Boss also knows that underlings who are well adjusted do not have any gripes or complaints. People who have their heads on straight just keep on doing whatever is required of them without question or contradiction.

Accordingly, the Real Boss tends to ignore protests of any kind. He surmises that the problem will go away if he ignores it long enough. Most likely the disgruntled employee only wants attention, in which case he'll soon realize he's wasting his time and stop grumbling.

Even if the grumbling doesn't stop, the Real Boss knows there is one sure solution: he can always transfer the employee to a job in which he'll be working for someone else.

"There seems to be an attitude problem, Sir."

Real Boss Views
on Training

As far as the Real Boss is concerned, few items in his annual budget are a bigger waste of money than training.

It's not that the Real Boss is opposed to training per se. What he opposes is any needless expenditure of time or money. And in his opinion, training is one thing that is always a complete waste of time *and* money.

After all, the Real Boss reasons, training certainly isn't called for in the case of anyone who knows how to do his or her job. This person needs only to be left alone to do it.

And training really can't be justified for anyone who *doesn't* know how to do his or her job. This person has no business spending time away from the job, for training or anything else. This person needs to spend as much time as possible *doing* the job, in order to learn how to do it better.

Training isn't even merited in the case of someone who wants to learn how to do some other job. When this person gets the other job, he'll have plenty of opportunity to learn how to do it. He won't need to know how to do it before then anyway. Besides, there's always the chance that this person won't *get* the other job. And in that case, he obviously doesn't need to know how to do it at all.

How the Real Boss Screens Potential Employees

Every Real Boss knows that the careful evaluation of potential employees is very important. While the proper person could turn out to be a big asset to the Real Boss as well as to the corporation, selection of a candidate who proves unsuitable could end up embarrassing the Real Boss and costing the corporation a great deal in terms of time and money. Thus the Real Boss always looks over all potential employees very carefully before deciding which person to hire.

The first thing the Real Boss considers in evaluating a potential employee is whether the person has any friends or relatives who are employed by the corporation in any positions that are superior in rank to his own. If the candidate has any friends or relatives who fall into this category, the Real Boss is quick to recognize that this candidate is decidedly the most suitable one for the job. No Real Boss can fail to realize that this candidate possesses the same high level of potential and many of the other excellent qualities that enabled the candidate's friend or relative to attain a position of such responsibility. And having found a person with this much promise, the Real Boss is spared the need to look further: the most qualified candidate clearly has been found.

However, should the Real Boss complete his screening of potential employees without finding anyone having suitable connections, he must then resort to other less valid criteria as his basis for selection. Under these circumstances, the Real Boss goes on to consider the length and style of the candidate's hair.

All Real Bosses realize that a lot can be learned about a person's character and political persuasions by looking at the person's hair style. The Real Boss knows that only hippies, drug freaks, communists, and other anti-establishment types sport long hair. Since this type of person is likely to sell the company's secrets to the Russians and commit other acts of sabotage, every Real Boss conscientiously avoids hiring anyone having long hair—unless, of course, the applicant is a female.

In fact, if the applicant is a female, the Real Boss actually will prefer that she have long hair. Not only is long hair on a female nice to look at, but it also indicates that the wearer is fairly conventional in her outlook on life. Long hair suggests to the Real Boss that a female will be so glad to have a job as something other than a teacher or a nurse that she'll be happy to work for a lower salary than that paid to males for doing the same job. Long hair also suggests that the applicant won't mind making the coffee each morning, or taking notes at all the meetings. Every Real Boss knows that women have much neater handwriting than do men— and they are also more likely to know shorthand.

All Real Bosses know that only women who are hard-nosed, bra-burning, women's liberation types are going to cut their hair short in an effort to look like men. This type of woman is likely to be independent and assertive, and the Real Boss realizes that a woman like that can only be a bad influence: before long, she's likely to have the other females in the office refusing to make coffee and take notes. No Real Boss is willing to encourage this kind of behavior, for it will require that his male employees assume some of those responsibilities traditionally assigned to the females. And that, in turn, will only cut into the organization's productivity and profit.

Besides, the Real Boss realizes that any female who goes to such lengths to look like a male will probably think she's qualified to handle the same jobs as the men, and that will never do. The Real Boss knows there are certain jobs that no woman can handle as well as a man. Women are too sentimental, too illogical, too inclined toward hysteria and other kinds of emotional instability on a fairly regular basis.

Of course, the Real Boss does recognize the importance of hiring enough females to fulfill his EEO quotas, since it is definitely in his best interests to do so. The Real Boss always hires the right number of women to do this, regardless of the kinds of jobs he has to give them. But whenever possible, he hires only the ones with long hair.

The Real Boss is also wary of hiring anyone who is going bald. The Real Boss knows that the ability to manage one's personal life is a valid indication of one's ability to manage one's professional responsibilities. Surely no one who is really in control of his or her life will allow the loss of his or her hair — unless this person is a communist or a hippie attempting to affect a disguise.

However, if the Real Boss is going bald, he might just be willing to overlook the fact that the applicant is doing likewise. In fact, this Real Boss might even prefer a candidate who is balding. Under these circumstances, the Real Boss is likely to consider hair loss to be a sign of intelligence and deep concern—and these are certainly qualities the Real Boss likes an employee to have.

The third thing a Real Boss considers in evaluating a potential employee is whether the candidate is clean-shaven. The Real Boss will sometimes overlook a neatly trimmed mustache on a candidate who satisfies all other requirements, but beards are definitely out. Not only do beards collect dust and germs, which makes them a health hazard to the whole organization, but they are also indicative of laziness. What else would prompt anyone to walk around looking so totally unkempt? Further, the Real Boss does not discriminate on this matter. This standard is applied with equal stringency to male and female candidates alike.

Fourth on the list of considerations is the candidate's footgear. Every Real Boss knows that any male candidate who expects to be considered seriously will be wearing shoes, and matched socks. However if the candidate's hair is short enough, the Real Boss will not rule out that candidate whose socks don't match—so long as both socks are the same color.

If the candidate is a female, the Real Boss will expect her to be wearing matched stockings as opposed to matched socks. However, the Real Boss will tolerate matched white tennis socks on a female if this applicant is also wearing a matched pair of running shoes. And the Real Boss fully approves of females wearing running shoes, since these shoes will enable them to get to the coffee machine that much faster when the pot is empty or in need of cleaning.

Whether a candidate's shoes match is very important. The Real Boss knows that anyone who fails to wear a matched pair of shoes to a job interview is not discerning enough to warrant further consideration. In addition, if the applicant is wearing shoes that require laces, the Real Boss will insist that these laces be present. The Real Boss will further insist that these laces match the shoes, and also that they match each other in terms of color and length. Lastly, the Real Boss will insist that these laces be tied, preferably in a bow. All Real Bosses realize that there is a very real correlation between a candidate's ability to lace and tie his shoes and that person's ability to reason things through in a logical manner. The Real Boss conscientiously shuns any candidate whose shoelaces are not tied, since this candidate is very likely to be deficient in terms of reasoning and analytical skills.

Likewise, the Real Boss is wary of any candidate wearing shoes that do not require laces. The Real Boss theorizes that anyone who wears shoes of this type probably does so deliberately in order to avoid having to figure out how to insert and tie these laces. The Real Boss knows that this person is likely not only to be deficient in the area of problem-solving skills, but also to be afraid of a challenge.

Once the Real Boss has finished appraising the candidate's socks and shoes, he goes on to consider the rest of this person's áttire. Male or female, the applicant is expected to be wearing a suit. The Real Boss always looks closely at the width of the lapels on this suit, and pays close attention to the color. Ideally, the suit will be navy blue, especially if the applicant is being considered for a job in sales. No Real Boss will ever hire for a sales position any applicant who does not look good in navy.

The Real Boss is also quick to notice whether the candidate is wearing a tie. All male candidates are expected to be wearing ties, though these ties should not be too wide or too colorful. However, the Real Boss is immediately wary of any female who is wearing a tie. The Real Boss realizes that any female who wears a tie is hungry for power, in which case she is probably after his job. Not that she could ever handle it, mind you.

If time permits, the Real Boss will then go on to consider such lesser factors as the candidate's educational background and related job experience. All other factors being equal—or even only slightly unequal—the Real Boss usually hires the person having the shortest hair and the most neatly tied shoelaces. Every Real Boss understands that short hair and neatly tied shoelaces are indicative of a positive attitude and an orderly mind, two qualities that go far toward predicting a person's success within the corporate environment. Besides, given these characteristics, the right person can always acquire the training and experience needed to do the job on the job as he does the job.

"Worst case of nepotism I've ever seen."

High Points In

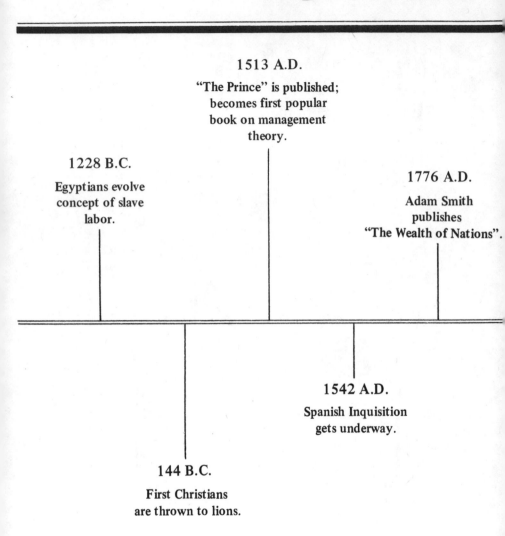

1513 A.D.

"The Prince" is published;
becomes first popular
book on management
theory.

1228 B.C.

Egyptians evolve
concept of slave
labor.

1776 A.D.

Adam Smith
publishes
"The Wealth of Nations".

1542 A.D.

Spanish Inquisition
gets underway.

144 B.C.

First Christians
are thrown to lions.

Real Boss History

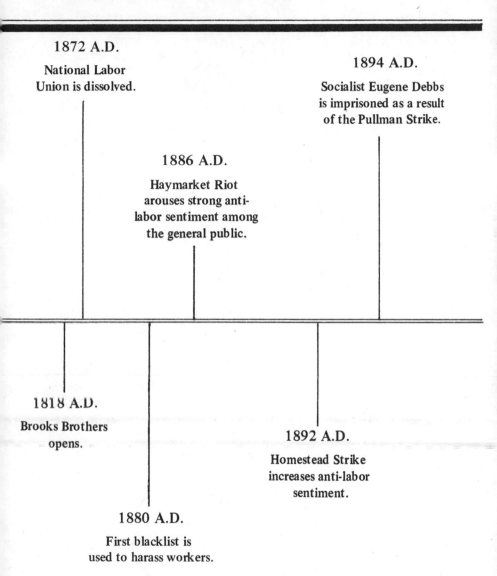

1872 A.D.

National Labor
Union is dissolved.

1894 A.D.

Socialist Eugene Debbs
is imprisoned as a result
of the Pullman Strike.

1886 A.D.

Haymarket Riot
arouses strong anti-
labor sentiment among
the general public.

1818 A.D.

Brooks Brothers
opens.

1892 A.D.

Homestead Strike
increases anti-labor
sentiment.

1880 A.D.

First blacklist is
used to harass workers.

High Points In

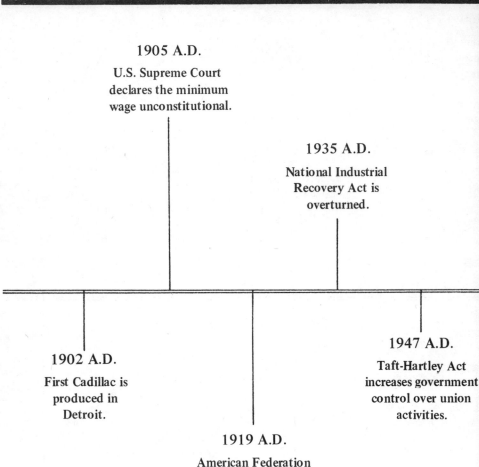

1905 A.D.

U.S. Supreme Court
declares the minimum
wage unconstitutional.

1935 A.D.

National Industrial
Recovery Act is
overturned.

1902 A.D.

First Cadillac is
produced in
Detroit.

1947 A.D.

Taft-Hartley Act
increases government
control over union
activities.

1919 A.D.

American Federation
of Labor fails in its
attempt to organize
steel workers.

Real Boss History

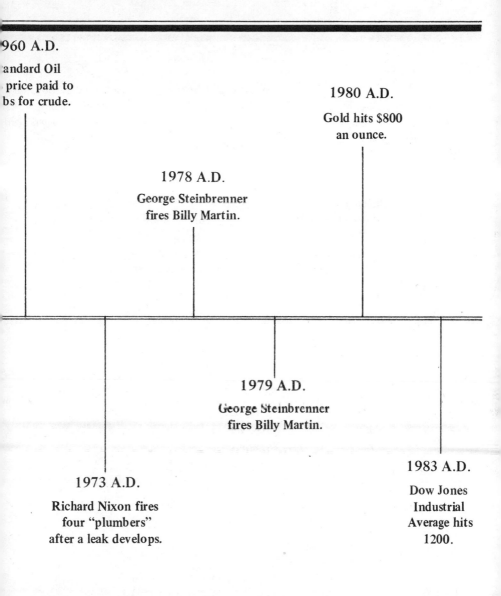

960 A.D.

andard Oil
price paid to
bs for crude.

1980 A.D.

Gold hits $800
an ounce.

1978 A.D.

George Steinbrenner
fires Billy Martin.

1979 A.D.

George Steinbrenner
fires Billy Martin.

1973 A.D.

Richard Nixon fires
four "plumbers"
after a leak develops.

1983 A.D.

Dow Jones
Industrial
Average hits
1200.

Low Points In

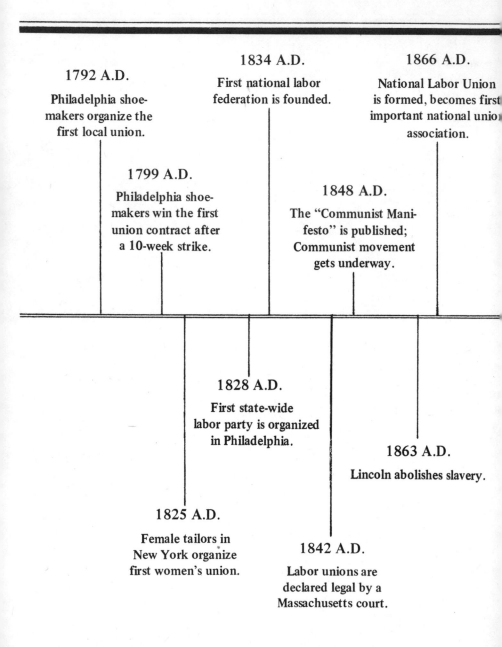

1792 A.D.

Philadelphia shoe-
makers organize the
first local union.

1834 A.D.

First national labor
federation is founded.

1866 A.D.

National Labor Union
is formed, becomes first
important national union
association.

1799 A.D.

Philadelphia shoe-
makers win the first
union contract after
a 10-week strike.

1848 A.D.

The "Communist Mani-
festo" is published;
Communist movement
gets underway.

1828 A.D.

First state-wide
labor party is organized
in Philadelphia.

1863 A.D.

Lincoln abolishes slavery.

1825 A.D.

Female tailors in
New York organize
first women's union.

1842 A.D.

Labor unions are
declared legal by a
Massachusetts court.

Real Boss History

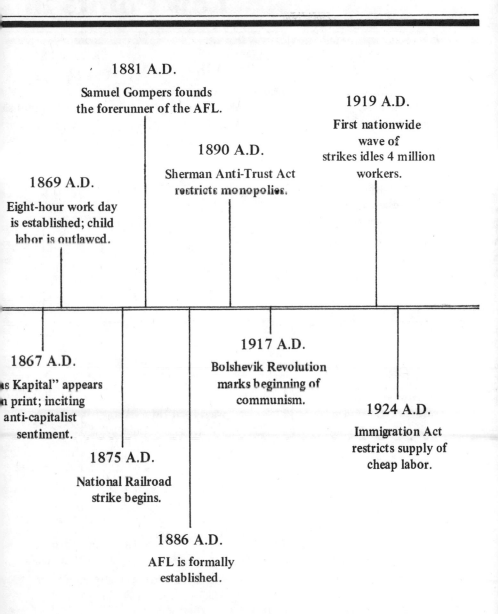

1881 A.D.

Samuel Gompers founds
the forerunner of the AFL.

1919 A.D.

First nationwide
wave of
strikes idles 4 million
workers.

1890 A.D.

Sherman Anti-Trust Act
restricts monopolies.

1869 A.D.

Eight-hour work day
is established; child
labor is outlawed.

1867 A.D.

as Kapital" appears
n print; inciting
anti-capitalist
sentiment.

1917 A.D.

Bolshevik Revolution
marks beginning of
communism.

1924 A.D.

Immigration Act
restricts supply of
cheap labor.

1875 A.D.

National Railroad
strike begins.

1886 A.D.

AFL is formally
established.

Low Points In

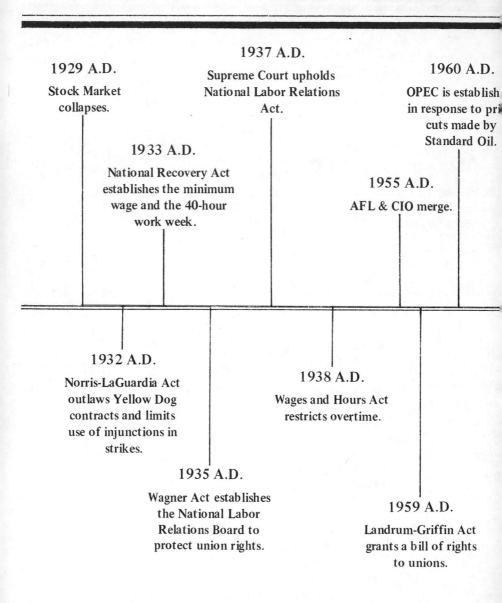

1929 A.D.

Stock Market
collapses.

1937 A.D.

Supreme Court upholds
National Labor Relations
Act.

1960 A.D.

OPEC is establish
in response to pri
cuts made by
Standard Oil.

1933 A.D.

National Recovery Act
establishes the minimum
wage and the 40-hour
work week.

1955 A.D.

AFL & CIO merge.

1932 A.D.

Norris-LaGuardia Act
outlaws Yellow Dog
contracts and limits
use of injunctions in
strikes.

1938 A.D.

Wages and Hours Act
restricts overtime.

1935 A.D.

Wagner Act establishes
the National Labor
Relations Board to
protect union rights.

1959 A.D.

Landrum-Griffin Act
grants a bill of rights
to unions.

Real Boss History

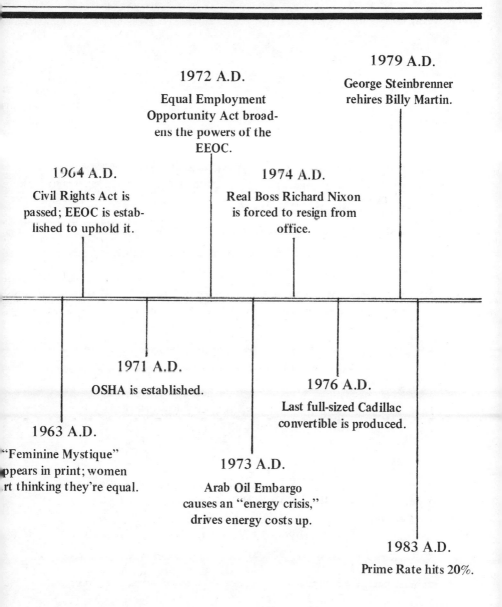

1979 A.D.

George Steinbrenner rehires Billy Martin.

1972 A.D.

Equal Employment Opportunity Act broadens the powers of the EEOC.

1964 A.D.

Civil Rights Act is passed; EEOC is established to uphold it.

1974 A.D.

Real Boss Richard Nixon is forced to resign from office.

1971 A.D.

OSHA is established.

1976 A.D.

Last full-sized Cadillac convertible is produced.

1963 A.D.

"Feminine Mystique" appears in print; women rt thinking they're equal.

1973 A.D.

Arab Oil Embargo causes an "energy crisis," drives energy costs up.

1983 A.D.

Prime Rate hits 20%.

Real Boss Review

1. Do you consistently forget your secretary's name?

2. Has the union local burned you in effigy at least once within the last year?

3. Do your plants wilt at the sound of your voice?

4. Have you fired at least five percent of your staff within the last six months?

5. Do you keep a written record of the number of minutes each of your subordinates takes for lunch each day?

6. Within the last twenty-four hours, have you ignored at least three of your subordinates when you've passed them in the hall?

7. Do you remember the exact date and time when your existing union contracts expire?

Scoring:

If you answered "YES" to all 7 questions, congratulations! You're a Real Boss! If you answered "YES" to 4–6 questions, you probably eat lunch with your subordinates. If you answered "YES" to 3 or fewer questions, you probably *are* one of your subordinates.

"I'm not in."

What the
Real Boss Reads

The Real Boss has very little time for any of those pursuits that are generally categorized as leisure activities. He's usually too busy trying to stay on top of his Real Boss duties to have much time to play.

Nonetheless, on occasion the Real Boss will manage to find some time for relaxation. When he does, he often uses this time to read.

For the most part, however, the Real Boss limits his reading materials to newspapers and magazines.* Not only are these periodicals always up-to-date but, in addition, the articles are fairly short. This enables the Real Boss to stay abreast of what's going on without having to invest a lot of time.

Very seldom does the Real Boss take the time out from his busy schedule to read an entire book. Most books require far more time than the Real Boss can spare. Besides, very few books in print today are relevant to his interests. Only when a book promises what he sees as valuable insights into the Real Boss world does the Real Boss feel that the book merits the time required to read it.

---

* The Real Boss's tastes in periodicals are fairly predictable: he sticks to the industrial and commercial journals. He will occasionally read the news weeklies, but that's about as frivolous as he'll get. He doesn't even bother with girlie magazines—the figures they show just aren't the kind he likes.

The Real Boss's Favorite Books *

Looking Out For Number One
Winning Through Intimidation
Standard and Poor's Index
Moneypower
How You Can Use Inflation to Beat the IRS
The Only Investment Guide You'll Ever Need
The Hard Money Book
The Inflation-Beater's Investment Guide
Spare-Time Steps to Your First Million
The Swiss Banking Handbook
Money Dynamics for the 1980's
William E. Donoghue's No-Load Mutual Fund Guide
How to Wake Up the Financial Genius Inside of You
Creating Wealth
Survive and Win in the Inflationary Eighties
New Profits from the Monetary Crisis
Financial Survival
Sylvia Porter's New Money Book for the 80's

---

* While it isn't one of his favorite books, the Real Boss's library also includes a copy of *The Prophet*. This was given to the Real Boss by a well-meaning friend who happened to be a very poor speller.

Books the Real Boss
Ought to Read —
But Won't

The New Rational Manager
Theory Z
The Art of Being a Boss
On Becoming a Person
Living, Loving, and Learning
How to Make Love to a Woman

Books the Real Boss Would Like to See Burned

The New Assertive Woman
Pulling Your Own Strings
Don't Say Yes When You Want to Say No
The Sky's The Limit
You Can If You Want To
Real Bosses Don't Say "Thank You"
Everything by Judith Krantz
Everything by Jacqueline Susann
Everything by Danielle Steel

Real Boss Fictional Heroes

The Real Boss virtually never reads fiction. Granted, Robert Ludlum and John LeCarre write great spy stories—but what can a spy story do for the bottom line?

Once upon a time, however—way back before he became a Real Boss—the Real Boss did read a fair amount of fiction. And in doing so, the Real Boss developed a healthy respect for many of the characters he encountered. He developed an especially strong admiration for those characters who epitomize all of the qualities Real Bosses hold so dear—those qualities so essential to being a Real Boss. In fact, it is often the behavior of these fictional heroes of his youth that the Real Boss uses as the model for his own behavior.

These fictional heroes include:

Captain Queeg, in *The Caine Mutiny*
Simon Legree, in *Uncle Tom's Cabin*
Richard III, in *King Richard the Third*
Ebenezer Scrooge, in *A Christmas Carol*
Claudius, in *Hamlet*
Alec d'Urberville, in *Tess of the d'Urbervilles*
Edmund, in *King Lear*
Don Corleone, in *The Godfather*
Heathcliff, in *Wuthering Heights*
Shylock, in *The Merchant of Venice*
The Sheriff of Nottingham, in *Robin Hood*
Captain Bligh, in *Mutiny on the Bounty*
Iago, in *Othello*
Fagin, in *Oliver Twist*
Uriah Heep, in *David Copperfield*

The Real Boss's Favorite Cartoon Character

Mr. Dithers, in *Dagwood Bumstead*

"Must you always bring your work home with you?"

Real Boss Food

What the Real Boss eats depends largely upon who is doing the cooking.

If the person doing the cooking happens to be the wife of *his* boss, the Real Boss eats whatever he's served — and *likes* it, no matter what it is or how it tastes.

Otherwise, the Real Boss generally eats whatever is quickest and most convenient. After all, food is merely a necessity to the Real Boss, a means of refueling his body in preparation for the many Real Boss tasks that lie ahead.

The Real Boss doesn't have time to ponder in detail the mysteries of an extensive menu. Invariably he is in a big hurry to get back to his Real Boss duties. As it is, he's sure to kill twenty minutes or more before he ever even orders his food. He usually takes at least that long to polish off his three martinis.

Booze and the Real Boss

An important part of maintaining a suitable Real Boss image is knowing just what—and where—to drink.

Being seen in the right watering holes—with the right people—is a must.

Equally important is knowing what drinks to order . . . and which drinks to avoid. Being seen with the wrong drink in one's hand can ruin the whole Real Boss effect.

Accordingly, the Real Boss is very particular about what he drinks and how he drinks it.

I. What the Real Boss Drinks

The Real Boss never drinks cream drinks of any kind. Cream drinks are for sissies and for little old ladies; they just don't command enough respect. The Real Boss knows that even a guy like J.R. Ewing would be laughed right out of Dallas if he were ever caught sipping a Sombrero. And can anyone honestly envision Billy Martin brawling at Regine's with a Pink Squirrel in hand?

(Actually, there is a second reason why the Real Boss never drinks cream drinks: he is not willing to be suspected of having an ulcer. For this would suggest that he can't handle the stresses associated with being a Real Boss. So the Real Boss smiles gamely—and follows his bourbon on the rocks with a double Alka-Seltzer.)

Likewise, the Real Boss steers clear of sweet drinks and fruity drinks. Ever the consummate capitalist, the Real Boss wants to be able to taste the stuff that's costing him three bucks a shot. He doesn't want the flavor masked by sweeteners or fruit juice. Besides, no Real Boss wants to be considered sweet—or fruity. Would a Real Boss like Blake Carrington risk his reputation by drinking a Colorado Boulevard in public — even in Denver? Is Bill Agee likely to celebrate his next take-over—or finding his next job—with a Crown Royal and

Seven-Up? And while "sweet" certainly isn't a word. that many people will ever apply to George Steinbrenner no matter what he drinks, can anyone really imagine him toasting a Yankee win with a Chivas Regal Sour?

Any Real Boss who seeks to emulate these giants of the corporate world learns early on that there are rules for drinking just as there are rules for everything else:

1. If you want to be seen as a strong boss, make sure you're seen drinking strong drinks.

2. If you want to be seen as successful—and every Real Boss does, for he knows that nothing succeeds like success—make sure you're seen drinking premium brands. ("It costs more," the Real Boss admits. "But I'm worth it.")

In keeping with these rules, the Real Boss can usually be found drinking one or more of the following:

Vodka:	Stolichnaya
Gin:	Beefeater or Tanqueray
Scotch:	Chivas Regal, Royal Salute, Johnny Walker Black Label, Glenlivet
Rye:	Crown Royal
Bourbon:	Jack Daniels
Brandy:	Remy Martin

II. How He Drinks It

Once the Real Boss has decided what to drink, he comes to the easy part: deciding how to drink it.

Over the years, Real Bosses of the world have come to prefer that their drinks be served in any of five ways:

A.   Straight Up

B.   On the Rocks

C.   With a twist of lemon

D.   With a wedge of lime

E.   All of the above

III. Exceptions to the Rule

If the Real Boss has high blood pressure, he may well opt for a glass of Perrier rather than anything alcoholic.

In keeping with his Real Boss image, however, the Real Boss does not let on that he is drinking Perrier. Instead, he usually throws three or four lime wedges into his drink—and then tries to pass it off as his fourth Vodka and Tonic.

"You might like to know, sir, that the vodka you're drinking was made from grain we shipped to the Soviet Union."

Notable Quotes From Real Boss Literature #1

"You thought!   You *thought!*   You're not being paid to think! ... You just do as you're goddamned told, and don't go thinking —*please!*"

The Caine Mutiny by Herman Wouk

Real Boss Television

The Real Boss doesn't watch a lot of television. There aren't too many shows the Real Boss likes. He'll occasionally watch a sporting event, such as a football game or a fight. As might be expected, the Real Boss likes anything that's highly competitive—contests where only one person or team can win.

And the Real Boss always watches the news. The Real Boss likes the news; he likes to know what's going on around him at all times. You can't be too well informed, the Real Boss reasons. (Besides, if a war is about to break out, he'll want as much advance notice as possible. He's got to buy into the steel companies early in order to make a decent profit.)

The Real Boss also watches shows that deal with finance or any other aspect of the business world. But aside from that, there's little that he'll watch.

However, the Real Boss does know what other shows are on the air, even if he doesn't watch any of them on a regular basis. After all, he had to watch each show once to decide he didn't like it.* And while he didn't find many shows he liked, he did come across a couple of notable characters.

---

* Actually, the Real Boss has never watched any of the soap operas. He figures maybe he'll try some of these after he retires. But he's not worried about missing out on any of the plot in the meantime. He's read enough about these soap operas to know that nothing will have happened by then anyway.

As you might have guessed, these characters include:

Blake Carrington, in *Dynasty*
J. R. Ewing, in *Dallas*
George Jefferson, in *The Jeffersons*
Mr. Slate, in *Fred Flintstone*
Archie Bunker, in *Archie's Place*
Ralph Cramden, in *The Honeymooners*
Mr. Hart, in *Nine to Five*
Mel, in *Alice*

The Real Boss's Ideal

	SUNDAY	MONDAY	TUESDAY
Daytime	Football		
6:00	Firing Line	MacNeil-Lehrer Newshour	MacNeil-Lehrer Newshour
6:30			
7:00	Face The Nation	Evening Report	Evening Report
7:30	Meet The Press	Wall Street Today	Wall Street Today
8:00	60 Minutes		
8:30		News Carnival	News Carnival
9:00	This Week	Movie: In High Places (1968)	Wall Street Blue
9:30	Last Week		Inside Business Today
10:00	Next Week		
10:30	Newsbeat		Night Newsline
11:00		11:00 News	11:00 News
11:30	News Wrap-Up	News Nightline	News Nightline
12:00	Wall Street Preview	Tomorrow's News Tonight	Tomorrow's News Tonight
12:30			

Television Schedule

EDNESDAY	THURSDAY	FRIDAY	SATURDAY
			Golf
cNeil-Lehrer ewshour	MacNeil-Lehrer Newshour	MacNeil-Lehrer Newshour	N. E. W. S.
			Spiderman
ening Report	Evening Report	Evening Report	Newsprobe
ll Street day	Wall Street Today	Wall Street Today	Newsbriefs
			Washington Week in Review
ws Carnival	News Carnival	Mid-Evening Report	Wall Street Week
ues & Answers	Basketball	Newsbeat	Movie: The High and The Mighty (1964)
siness Finale		Festival of News	
ght Newsline		Night Newsline	
:00 News	11:00 News	11:00 News	11:00 News
ws Nightline	News Nightline	News Nightline	Saturday News Live
morrow's ws Tonight	Tomorrow's News Tonight	Tomorrow's News Tonight	Late Evening Report
			$ NEWS $

"And now, to present the civilian point of view, the president of the Globex Chemical and Arms Corporation."

Real Boss
Words of Wisdom #6

"Damn the torpedoes — full speed ahead."

—Admiral Farragut

Real Boss Music

The Real Boss spends very little time listening to music. Why should he listen to music when he could be listening to the latest Dow Jones report —or eavesdropping on someone else's conversation with E. F. Hutton?

When he does listen to music, the Real Boss usually limits himself to serious, respectable music—something classical, perhaps, or maybe an opera.

Very little attention does any Real Boss pay to most of the pop music that reverberates across the airwaves today. As far as the Real Boss is concerned, the Top Fifty are ranked by *Fortune*, not the local disk jockey.

And rock groups? Those are something the Real Boss once studied in Geology class.

Real Boss Rock

Yet in all fairness to the Real Boss, it must be noted that not *all* of the current rock groups are completely unknown to him; he does recognize a *few* of the names he hears bandied about by the deejays.

For example, he certainly knows who the Eagles are. He even watches some of their games.

And how could he ever forget Men at Work? That's a sight the Real Boss loves to see.

Air Supply? That's a company in Altoona that manufactures oxygen tanks. At one time, the Real Boss owned more than 50 shares in this company.

Chicago is where the Real Boss changes planes. Creedence Clearwater is where he might live after he retires.

Asia? That's a large continent just off the coast of Japan.

Menudo is a quaint little Spanish restaurant in Scarsdale.

Blondie is Dagwood's wife.

Bread is what the Real Boss uses to hold peanut butter and jelly together.

Toto? That was the little dog in *The Wizard of Oz*.

And Police? That's what the Real Boss watches out for as he's speeding off to a meeting.

The Real Boss's Favorite Song

My Way, by Frank Sinatra

Notable Quotes
From Real Boss
Literature #2

"I fired Newkirk on the spot. Nobody slugs a foreman around here and gets away with it."

Wheels, by Arthur Hailey

Real Boss Sports

Real Boss participation in sports rarely extends beyond reaching over to the television set to tune in the Sunday afternoon football game or the evening's double-header. The Real Boss will occasionally watch sports, but he is not likely to become actively involved in most of them. It's just not seemly for one of the captains of industry to be seen rolling around in the dirt, getting his Brooks Brothers shirt all wrinkled. For this reason, football, baseball, soccer, hockey, and all of the other rough sports are out.

However, the Real Boss does occasionally participate in some of the more gentlemanly sports. It's not uncommon for the Real Boss to be seen pitching horseshoes, throwing darts, taking a sauna bath, or getting a Swedish massage. And when it seems politically astute for him to do so, the Real Boss may even get into tennis or golf.

It isn't that the Real Boss especially enjoys these sports. How seriously can any Real Boss take a sport that uses terms like "love" to describe the score?

But it is good for his image to be seen driving up to the local country club—even if he never takes his golf clubs out of the trunk once he gets there. Besides, there's no telling who he'll meet. And there's always the chance he'll pick up a few good stock tips in the locker room.

"It's nice to get out and get some exercise after
sitting all day in the office."

The Real Boss's Favorite Game

Monopoly

Real Boss
Words of Wisdom #7

"Winning isn't everything. It's the only thing."

—Vince Lombardi

What the Real Boss Wears

The Real Boss is careful to dress at all times in a manner befitting his corporate image. Accordingly, the Real Boss generally dresses very conservatively. During business hours, he can usually be found in a dark suit (with narrow lapels), a blue or white shirt, and a club tie. He will also be wearing a matched pair of dark socks, and matched shoes: wing tips. With matched laces. Tied.

When the Real Boss is away from the office, he is only slightly less conservative in his choice of clothes. (After all, there is no telling when he might run into somebody from the office; one can't be too careful.) Under these circumstances, you may well find the Real Boss in a pair of tailored slacks and a sweater. But, while he probably won't be wearing wing tips, neither is he likely to be wearing sneakers. (The Real Boss knows well the old adage about guilt by association.)

Occasionally, you may even venture upon a Real Boss who sports blue jeans during leisure hours. However, it's a fairly safe bet that these are not designer jeans. The Real Boss knows that his own initials are enough. (Besides, the Real Boss rationalizes, had his parents wanted him to go through life with "Calvin Klein" plastered across his backside, they would have had the sense to name him Calvin Klein.)

Ten Things You'll Never Find in the Real Boss's Wardrobe

Designer labels

Floral prints

Leisure suits

Velour

Safari suits

Brocade

Metallic fabrics *

Bracelets *

Medallions *

Gold or silver chains *

---

* It isn't that the Real Boss is opposed to *buying* precious metals. He just doesn't believe in *wearing* them.

"Shall we try it on for corporate image?"

Notable Quotes From Real Boss Literature #3

"Let me hear another sound from *you,*" said Scrooge, "and you'll keep your Christmas by losing your situation."

A Christmas Carol by Charles Dickens

Sex and
the Real Boss

(No, folks, we didn't omit anything.)

"Do you know 'Money Makes the World Go 'Round'?"

A Profile of the Real Boss's

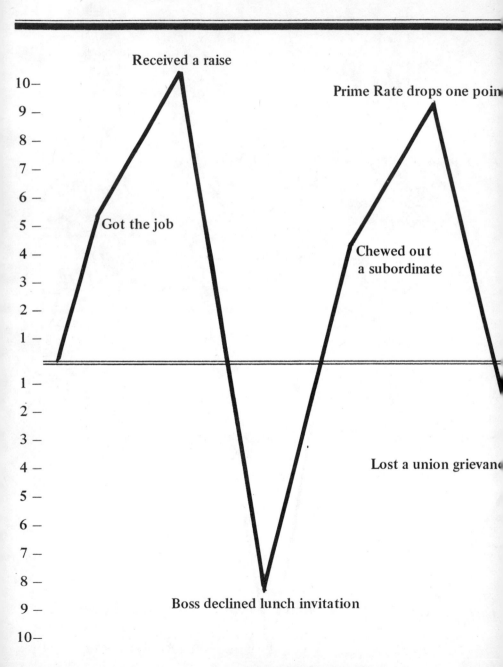

Received a raise

Prime Rate drops one poin[t]

10—
9 —
8 —
7 —
6 —
5 —   Got the job
4 —   Chewed out
3 —   a subordinate
2 —
1 —

1 —
2 —
3 —
4 —   Lost a union grievan[ce]
5 —
6 —
7 —
8 —
9 —   Boss declined lunch invitation
10—

Sexual Satisfaction

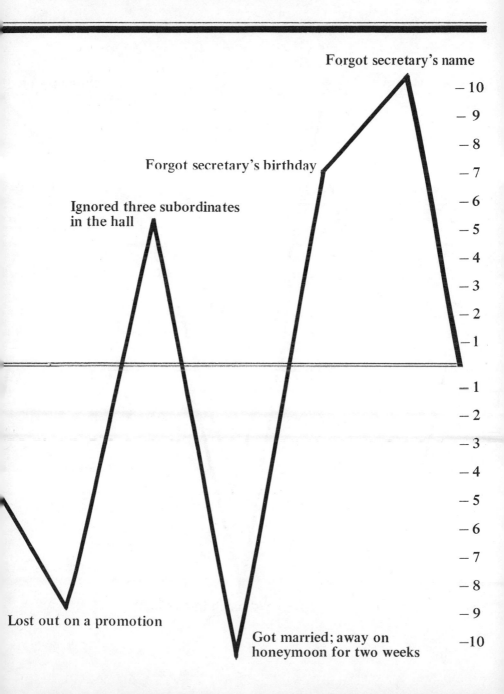

Forgot secretary's name

Forgot secretary's birthday

Ignored three subordinates
in the hall

Lost out on a promotion

Got married; away on
honeymoon for two weeks

- 10
- 9
- 8
- 7
- 6
- 5
- 4
- 3
- 2
- 1

- 1
- 2
- 3
- 4
- 5
- 6
- 7
- 8
- 9
- 10

A Profile of the Real Boss's

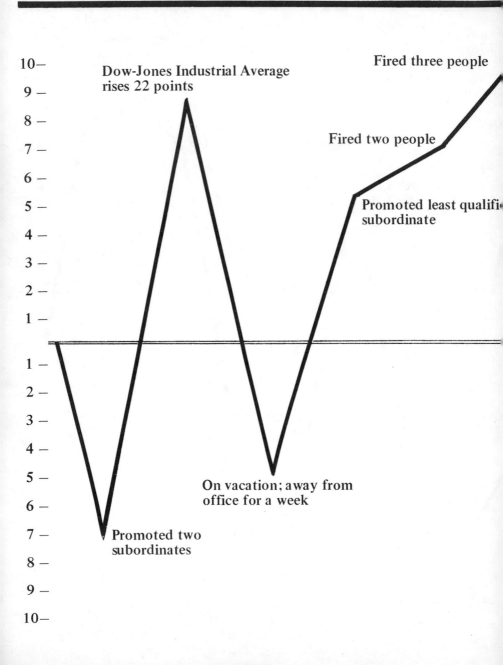

Dow-Jones Industrial Average
rises 22 points

Fired three people

Fired two people

Promoted least qualifi(
subordinate

10 —
9 —
8 —
7 —
6 —
5 —
4 —
3 —
2 —
1 —

1 —
2 —
3 —
4 —
5 —
6 —
7 —
8 —
9 —
10 —

On vacation; away from
office for a week

Promoted two
subordinates

Sexual Satisfaction

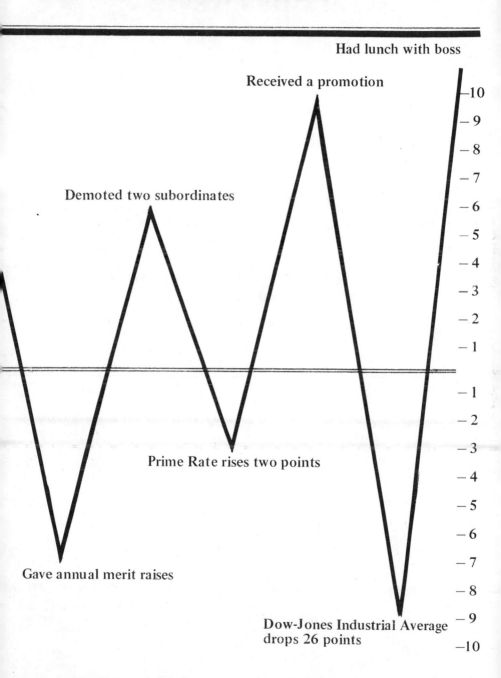

Real Boss Review

Q: What is the Real Boss's idea of successful foreplay?

A: One takeover, two mergers, and a Dow Jones closing average of at least 1000.

Motoring and the Real Boss

During the last hundred years, many devices have been invented that have made the life of a Real Boss a much easier one. Automatic redialing, the electric pencil sharpener, and the paper shredder all have done wonders to increase the efficiency of the Real Boss and his staff. But as useful as these things are, there is no invention for which the Real Boss is more grateful than the automobile.

Were it not for the automobile, Real Bosses over the years would have had to resort to the use of public transportation in order to travel back and forth to their offices each day and to scurry off to their meetings. And this would have caused the Real Boss no end of inconvenience. For public transportation offers the Real Boss very little flexibility in terms of where he can go and when he can get there. Needless to say, no Real Boss likes this. In addition, the use of public transportation requires that the Real Boss stand, often for hours, elbow to elbow with the common hordes. No Real Boss will *tolerate* this.

But the automobile is more than just a utility to the Real Boss, more than just a means of getting to meetings on time. In the eyes of the Real Boss, an automobile is a portable office—a vehicular think tank in which he can collect and analyze his thoughts as he heads from his home to the office (or vice versa, if it's the other way around).

For this reason, the Real Boss gives a great deal of thought to what kind of car he should own. The Real Boss wants a car that can provide him with the comfort and convenience he needs to carry out his Real Boss duties on the road. Yet he also wants a car that befits his status as a Real Boss. For the Real Boss's car is also an ego extension, an announcement to the world that its owner is in fact a Real Boss—a person of consequence within the corporate community.

Finding a car that can fill this bill is certainly not easy. Fortunately, the Real Boss knows just how to do so.

The first thing a Real Boss considers in buying a car is its size. The Real Boss wants a *big* car—a car that will let the world know its owner is a *big deal*. Real Bosses know that small cars just don't convey the appropriate degree of status. How can the Real Boss hope to command any respect if he's seen riding around in a Pinto, or a Chevette, or even a Volkswagen Rabbit? And surely no one can imagine a Real Boss trying to impress *his* boss by taking him out to lunch in a Plymouth Champ—unless his boss happens to be Lee Iacocca. In fact, the only small car any Real Boss will even consider buying is the Mercedes 380 SL. In this case, the Real Boss knows that the *price* is big enough to impress people even if the *car* isn't.

(Actually, the lack of status is not the only reason why the Real Boss steers clear of small cars. Another problem with small cars is that they just aren't practical. How can any Real Boss seriously consider owning a car that doesn't allow room for his bulging briefcase—to say nothing of his golf clubs?)

The Real Boss also wants a comfortable, luxurious car, because he doesn't like to be uncomfortable—although he has no qualms about making his underlings feel this way. For this reason, any car the Real Boss chooses will be spacious and will come equipped with every extra in the book.

Lastly, the Real Boss usually wants an American-made car. He believes American businessmen should stick together.

On the basis of these requirements, the Real Boss is generally found in one of three kinds of cars: a Cadillac, a Lincoln, or a Chrysler New Yorker. But there are some exceptions to these rules. An occasional Real Boss has been seen in an Oldsmobile, or a Buick, or even a Mercury Marquis. (In fact, in New Jersey a Real Boss was once spotted riding around in a full-size Chevrolet. Luckily, this happens only in New Jersey.) And once in a very great while, the Real Boss will even swallow his patriotism long enough to buy a foreign car. When he does, he will usually insist upon a full-size Mercedes if not a Rolls Royce.* (Real Boss imports are limited to those manufactured in Germany, Sweden, England and France. Under no circumstances does the Real Boss buy anything Japanese.)

Once the Real Boss has decided what kind of car to buy, he must then decide upon the color. Fortunately, this is easy. Being a serious, responsible person, the Real Boss sticks to serious, responsible colors: black, brown, burgundy, dark blue, and dark green.

If he's feeling particularly light-hearted—for a Real Boss, that is—he may even settle upon something in gray, silver, or white. But that's about as frivolous as the Real Boss ever gets. He conscientiously avoids cars that are painted red, yellow, orange, pink, purple, or any shade of pastel. No self-respecting Real Boss wants to be seen in a car that's painted the color of a school bus

---

* It should be noted that, while he will occasionally buy a *foreign* car, the Real Boss virtually never buys a *sports* car. And why should he? The Real Boss certainly isn't a very good *sport* .

or a fire engine—or worse still, an Easter Egg—regardless of the fancy names these colors are given. And who can blame him? How much respect would Al Capone have gotten if he had ridden around Chicago in a canary yellow Cadillac? And does anyone remember J. Edgar Hoover riding around Washington in a lavender Lincoln?

For that matter, the Real Boss doesn't even like such innocuous colors as tan or beige. These colors just aren't forceful enough for the Real Boss; they aren't suitably expressive of his personality. Besides, the Real Boss knows that tan and beige are the colors people buy when they're too lazy to get their cars washed on a regular basis. And the last thing any Real Boss wants to be considered is *lazy*.

"The price is only thirty-one thousand dollars, but the snob value is at least seventy-three thousand."

The Annual
S.O.B. Award

Once each year, the Society of Bosses (S.O.B.) meets to select the boss who has proven to be most worthy of induction into that illustrious and august body, the Real Boss Hall of Fame.

The person chosen is usually that boss who best typifies the ideal Real Boss—that person who has done the most during the last year to perpetuate those standards so highly revered by other Real Bosses throughout the world. Past winners of this prestigious award include such notables as:

— Monroe Rathbone, who, as Chairman of the Board of Standard Oil, in 1960 lowered the price paid to the Arabs per barrel of crude by 10 cents,

— Nelson Rockefeller, for the no-nonsense manner in which he dealt with the Attica uprising, and also for his official sanctioning of what has since come to be known as the "Rockefeller Salute," *

— Bill Agee, who perfected the notion of the "golden parachute" just before he had to bail out of Bendix,

---

* It should be noted that Mr. Rockefeller was nominated again in 1978, on the basis of the tremendous amount of overtime he so relentlessly required of his staff members—especially certain females. However, he did not receive the award that year; instead it was granted to the Shah of Iran.

- George Steinbrenner, for his steadfast refusal to re-hire Reggie Jackson despite the Yankees' apparent difficulty in winning a pennant without Jackson, and also for his constant attempts to intimidate Billy Martin,

- Billy Martin, for his persistent refusal to let the press—or George Steinbrenner—intimidate him.

So who is the most recent winner? Who will be the recipient of this coveted award for this past year? None other than James Watt, U.S. Secretary of the Interior and Guardian of the Nation's Virtue. Mr. Watt was selected not only on the basis of his impeccable taste in music and his deep concern for his country's moral well-being, but also for the uncanny foresight he has shown in recognizing the considerable economic advantage to be realized by cutting down much of the prime timber found in the nation's parklands and other wilderness areas. There can be no doubt that Mr. Watt's refusal to be swayed by environmentalists or even the considerable sentiment evoked by an eighty-year tradition of conservation has earned him a special place in the hearts of Real Bosses throughout the land — and many other Americans as well.

In recognition of this honor, Mr. Watt will receive the S.O.B. trophy, suitably engraved with his now-immortal words: "If you've seen one tree, you've seen them all."

Notable Quotes From Real Boss Literature #4

"... If you let up the pressure even once, your whole goddamn organization is apt to blow up in your face."

The Caine Mutiny by Herman Wouk

One Last Word
on Being
A Real Boss

I t is 5:15 p.m. You have had a long, exhausting day. You have spent the entire afternoon chewing out Gridlock, one of your subordinates, as a result of the proposal he has just presented. Despite the fact that Gridlock spent three whole months preparing this proposal, you can see no merit in it whatsoever — although you can see a great many flaws. Needless to say, you have been careful to point out each of these flaws to Gridlock, in front of all of his peers. You finished up by informing Gridlock that he is to redo the proposal in its entirety before he goes home tonight.

You pick up your briefcase and head for the door. As you do so, the telephone rings. Thinking it might be your broker calling to report the latest additions to your stock portfolio, you answer it. The caller turns out to be *your* boss. He knew Gridlock's proposal was due today, and he wants to hear all about it.

You tell him about Gridlock's proposal in detail. Before you have the chance to tell him your reactions to the proposal, he interrupts to give you *his* reactions: he thinks the proposal is terrific! In fact, he is so impressed by the proposal that he wants you to implement it at once.

You assure your boss that you agree with him 100%, and that you will take steps to implement the proposal first thing tomorrow. You then put down your briefcase, and set off to find Gridlock to tell him to go on home.

After all, being a Real Boss means knowing just when to be flexible.